Signing with Khy

Khyiana Tate

Published by: Sprouting Sunflowers LLC.
Copyrights©2021 Khyiana Tate, All Rights Reserved
Book Title: Signing with Khy
Date Published: December 2021
ISBN: 978-1-7349639-5-3

This book was published in the United States of America.
Developed & Accredited by: Sprouting Sunflowers LLC.

Sproutingsunflowers.com

This book is dedicated to my mom and in
honor of my grandmother Naomi!

I also dedicate this book to
the Deaf and Hard of Hearing.
We can do anything we want
to….except hear.

A

B

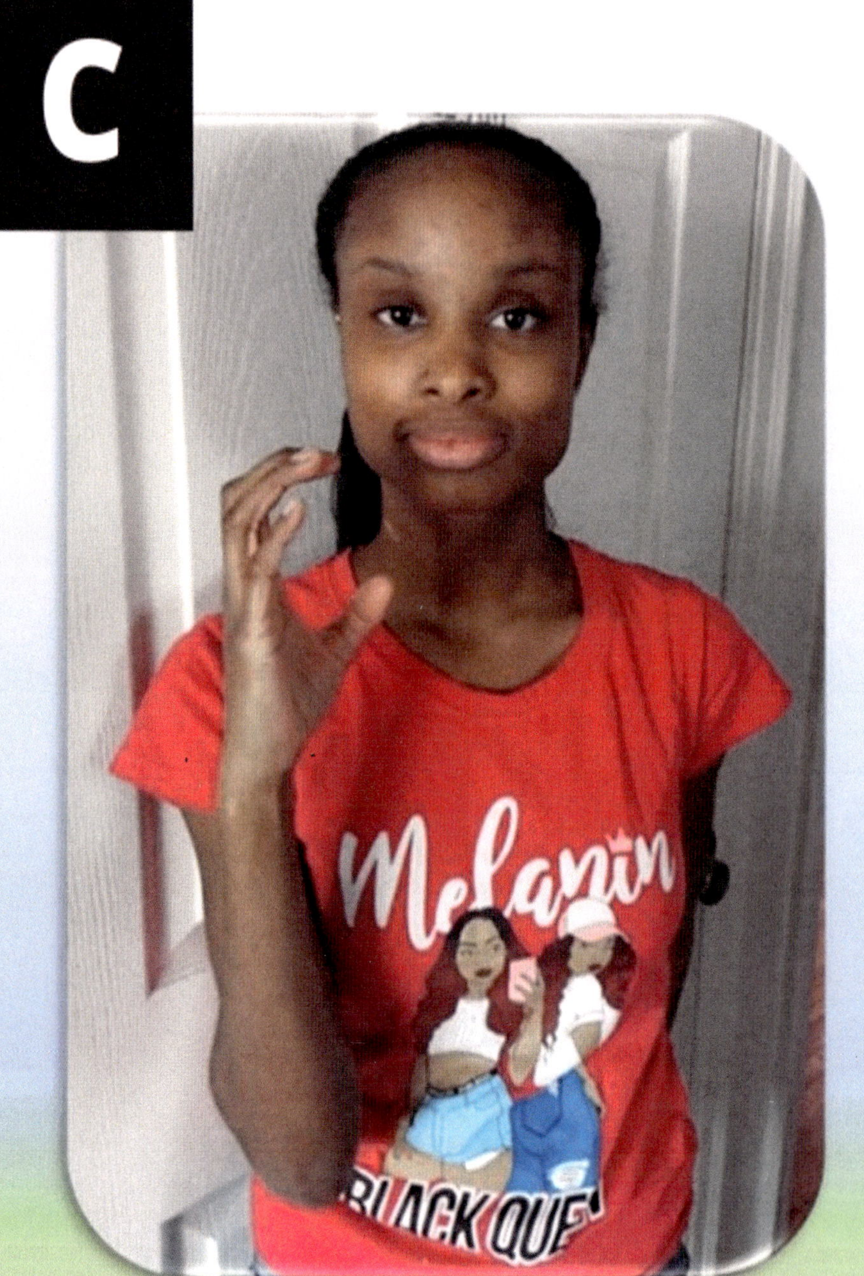
Melanin
BLACK QUE

D

E

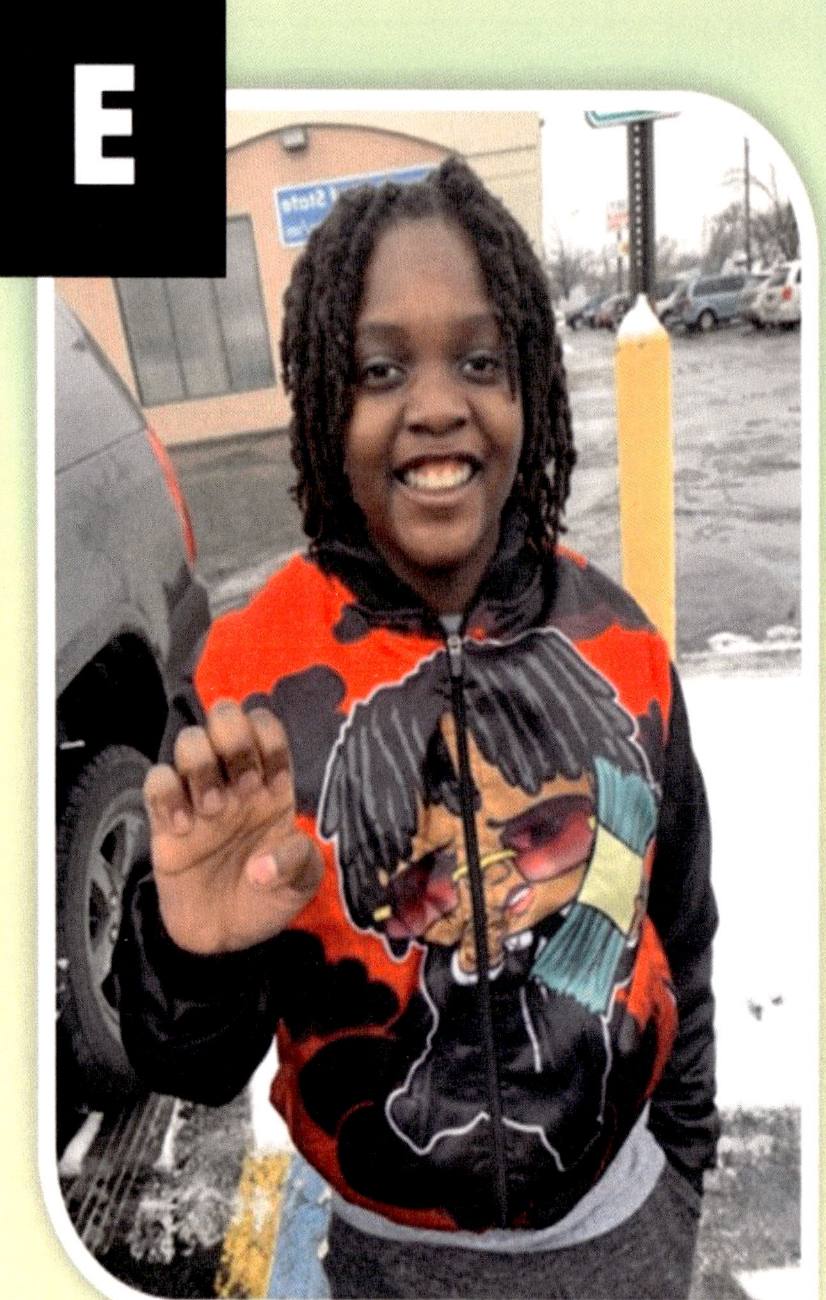

F

G

H

I

J

K

L

M
WE SAY I'M
WE ARE FAM

N
FIERCE

O

P

Q

R

MIAMI BEACH
FLORIDA

T

U

V

W

X

Y

Z

About the Author

Khyiana is a Deaf teen, born and raised in Detroit, Michigan. She does not let her Deafness stop her. She never takes no for an answer. Khyiana is always making sure the community is aware of Deaf Culture. She enjoys school and making others laugh. Her dream is to publish a book series, own her own hair salon, and to continue teaching sign language to the hearing community.

She's breaking statistics by proving that young Deaf women can be successful. Her goal is to bring awareness to sign language so that everyone can be able to communicate with each other. It is her desire that this book will build skills needed to understand the basic alphabet in order to be ready to go and learn more for better communication in sign language.

SIGNING WITH KHY

Made in the USA
Monee, IL
25 February 2022

91723943R00021